THE PERFECT CRIME

THE REAL-LIFE CRIME THAT INSPIRED HITCHCOCK'S ROPE

STRANGER THAN FICTION SERIES #5

FERGUS MASON

Absolute Crime Press
ANAHEIM, CALIFORNIA

Copyright © 2020 by Golgotha Press, Inc.

All rights reserved. No part of this publication may be reproduced, distributed or transmitted in any form or by any means, including photocopying, recording, or other electronic or mechanical methods, without the prior written permission of the publisher, except in the case of brief quotations embodied in critical reviews and certain other noncommercial uses permitted by copyright law.

Limited Liability / Disclaimer of Warranty. While best efforts have been used in preparing this book, the author and publishers make no representations or warranties of any kind and assume no liabilities of any kind with respect to accuracy or completeness of the content and specifically the author nor publisher shall be held liable or responsible to any person or entity with respect to any loss or incidental or consequential damages caused or alleged to have been caused, directly, or indirectly without limitations, by the information or programs contained herein. Furthermore, readers should be aware that the Internet sites listed in this work may have changed or disappeared. This work is sold with the understanding that the advice inside may not be suitable in every situation.

Trademarks. Where trademarks are used in this book this infers no endorsement or any affiliation with this book. Any trademarks (including, but not limiting to, screenshots) used in this book are solely used for editorial and educational purposes.

Contents

About Absolute Crime 7
Introduction: Death of A Schoolboy 9
   Chicago - May 21, 1924 9
Early Lives 13
   Nathan Leopold 13
   Richard Loeb 18
University 23
   Enter the Supermen 26
The Slippery Slope 29
The Murder of Robert Franks 36
Cleaning Up 52
Errors, Suspicions, and Arrests 60
Overwhelmed By Evidence 76
The Trial of the Century 80
Prison 94
Later Life 99
Conclusion 102
Ready for More? 107
   The True Story Behind Alfred Hitchcock's Psycho . 107
   The True Story Behind Alfred Hitchcock's The Birds
   107

Exposing Jack the Stripper: A Biography of the Worst Serial Killer You've Probably Never Heard Of 108

The Sapphire Affair: The True Story Behind Alfred Hitchcock's Topaz 109

The True Story Behind Alfred Hitchcock's The Wrong Man 110

Newsletter Offer *111*

About Absolute Crime

Absolute Crime publishes only the best true crime literature. Our focus is on the crimes that you've probably never heard of, but you are fascinated to read more about. With each engaging and gripping story, we try to let readers relive moments in history that some people have tried to forget.

Remember, our books are not meant for the faint at heart. We don't hold back--if a crime is bloody, we let the words splatter across the page so you can experience the crime in the most horrifying way!

If you enjoy this book, please visit our homepage (www.AbsoluteCrime.com) to see other books we offer; if you have any feedback, we'd love to hear from you!

Sign up for our mailing list, and we'll send you out a free true crime book!

http://www.absolutecrime.com/newsletter

Introduction: Death of a Schoolboy

Chicago - May 21, 1924

It was nearly 5:30 and Bobby Franks, walking briskly down Ellis Avenue, was late. He was supposed to be home by five on a school day, but he had a habit of letting the time run away from him. The 14-year-old had been in Dutch with his parents a few times already this year and didn't want another talking to from his father. Even more, he didn't want to have to look at the disappointed look on his mother's face again. They didn't exactly watch the clock, though, and usually allowed a bit of slack. Nothing would be said if he was home before dinner, he hoped.

Bobby really hadn't meant to be late, but like he often did he'd joined a pickup baseball game after class. The Harvard School, a private prep school in Chicago's up market Kenwood district, was popular with local Jewish families. Bobby's parents were converts to Christian Science, and not all that popular in the neighborhood, but he'd never had any trouble fitting in. It was a good school and the tutors were happy to supervise games after the last bell rang, even on an unseasonably cool day like this, but that didn't help Bobby's timekeeping. Still, he lived on the corner of Ellis and 51st and he was nearly at 49th already. He could make it in five minutes.

Just before he reached the junction of 49th he heard a shout, "Hey, Bob!" Turning, he saw a green Willys-Knight tourer at the curb; in the back seat he recognized Dick Loeb, an acquaintance whose family socialized with his own. "Want a ride home?" Loeb called.

Franks thought for a moment. He'd been taught not to take rides from strangers, and although Loeb wasn't a stranger - Bobby sometimes played tennis with him on the court at his house - wasn't there something just a little bit creepy about him? Anyway it was only a block and a half to his home and while cool the weather was dry. He shook his head. "Thanks, but I'd just as soon walk."

Loeb insisted. "Jump in for a minute anyway. I want to ask you about that tennis racket you've been using. I'm thinking of getting one for my brother Tommy."

Well, that seemed harmless enough. Bobby replied, "Sure, I guess," and walked over to the car. "You know Babe?" Loeb asked, waving a hand towards the driver. "Bobby, this is Nate Leopold. Nate, my good friend Bobby Franks." Bobby said hi to Leopold, and then climbed into the front seat; Leopold reached over and closed the door. "We'll just take a turn round the block while we talk, OK?" In front Leopold eased off the clutch and the Willys-Knight pulled away from the curb.

Bobby waited for Loeb to start talking about the racket, but the young man said nothing. He seemed almost expectant, as if he was waiting for something. Bobby felt sudden unease. These guys were creepy sure enough, and maybe he'd been right first time. He remembered some of the rumors at school about how Loeb and a friend - maybe this Leopold - were queer for each other. It might have been better to stay out of the car. Surely they wouldn't do anything right here in the street, though. Then, as Leopold turned left down 50th, he realized that the curtains were up on the side windows. He barely had time for that to sink in when Loeb calmly leaned forward and clamped a hand over his mouth.

Bobby Franks, numb with disbelief, sat helplessly as Loeb brought his hand up. He waited for whatever came next.

[1]
EARLY LIVES

Nathan Leopold

On November 19, 1904 Nathan Freudenthal Leopold, Junior was born in Chicago to a wealthy family of German immigrants. As was normal among the children of the very rich at the time his parents played a small part in his childhood, and much of his upbringing was left to a series of nurses and governesses. The traditionalist Leopold family favored European girls for these positions, and the young Leopold and his brothers Samuel and Foreman were raised in an environment where German was routinely spoken. Leopold's first words, spoken at the age of only four months, were "Nein, nein. Mama." His nurse at the time, and for the first five years of his life, was Marie Giessler, known as Mimie.

The Nathan Leopold that Mimie looked after was a small child, but it was already becoming clear that he was an exceptional one. Socially inept and physically awkward, Leopold showed well above average intelligence and quickly began to develop a wide range of interests.

When Leopold was five Mimie left the household and was replaced by Pauline Van den Bosch, a devout Christian who began teaching the boy about the saints. Leopold took to the subject with enthusiasm and used his wealthy background to advantage; he would get the family chauffeur to drive him around the neighborhood's churches looking for information on saints, and then worked on separating them into categories. Van den Bosch also taught Leopold about Jesus Christ and his crucifixion, which fascinated him. He later said, "The idea of nailing somebody to something was very appealing to me."[1] Van den Bosch only stayed for six months, but her influence had given Leopold new interests and new influences.

In Van den Bosch's place the Leopolds hired Mathilda Wantz, an immigrant from Alsace who spoke only German. Very different from her devout predecessor, Wantz - who Leopold nicknamed Sweetie - was manipulative and devious. She formed a complex relationship with the boys, and while it is hard to blame Leopold's later behavior on her influence she certainly didn't teach him the virtues of honesty. On one occasion she caught him stealing stamps from a cousin. Instead of punishing him or telling his parents she blackmailed him, using her knowledge to get extra days off which Leopold covered up for. She also bathed nude with the boys and wrestled with them as a reward when they behaved well. Finally, when Leopold was twelve and suffering from an illness, his mother caught Wantz dumping him out of his bed and she was dismissed.

Leopold had a difficult school career. He started off at Miss Spade's, a small private school that had started out co-ed but by the time Leopold got there was almost all female; only one other boy attended. There was a method in this, although it probably counts as madness too; Leopold's mother had noticed that he had difficulty making friends with girls, and decided that going to a girls' school would "cure him." It didn't. After two years he moved to the Douglas School. This was a public school and his social class made it tough to fit in. The fact that his mother told him not to touch anything or use the bathrooms there probably didn't help. Nobody else at Douglas lived on the exclusive Michigan Avenue, and none of them were walked to and from school by a governess every day, either. He was bullied by some of the other boys, who terrorized him when Wantz didn't arrive to walk him home.2 He had such a bad time there that he returned to Miss Spade's for the rest of the year.3

When Leopold was eight the family moved from Michigan Avenue to the Kenwood district. Their new address was only a block down from the private Harvard School, and Leopold was enrolled there. This got him away from the bullies, but he still wasn't very popular. His nicknames included "Flea" and "Crazy Bird" as well as the sarcastic "The Great Nathan."

When Leopold was 17 his mother died of nephritis. As her health had never recovered after giving birth to him he blamed himself, which only made his feelings about women more complicated.

Leopold had several hobbies, and one of them was ornithology. He had a genuine talent for it. With his intelligence and attention to detail the study of birds suited him well, and like most 1920s ornithologists he enthusiastically collected specimens. Modern bird watchers are happy to watch through binoculars and take photos with a telephoto lens; Leopold preferred a shotgun. He built a collection of over 3,000 specimens in his study at home, including many rare species.

Leopold knew - and shot - many birds, but he had a specialist subject, too. That was the Kirtland's Warbler. Setophaga Kirtlandii is a small brown bird with a yellow breast, which spends the winter in the Bahamas and the summer in a small area of Michigan, and in the 1920s it was declining fast. In fact by the early

1970s it was almost extinct, although numbers are now recovering. The danger to the Warbler wasn't Nathan Leopold's shotgun; it's now known that it was changing climate, which moved the Jack Pine forests whose seeds it depended on for food north. The surviving population was trapped on the Northern Peninsula and people didn't understand why they were dying out. If anyone did know it was Leopold; by 1923 he probably knew more about Kirtland's Warbler than anyone else on earth. In October of that year he travelled to Boston to present a paper on the bird to the American Ornithological Society's annual meeting.[4] It was an astounding achievement for an 18-year-old. For anyone else the respect and attention it gained would have been more than enough, but Leopold now cared more about impressing his college friend Richard Loeb.

Richard Loeb

Richard Albert Loeb was born on June 11, 1905. His parents, like Leopold's, were wealthy; his father Albert had started out as a lawyer but later became vice president of Sears and Roebuck. Albert and Anna Loeb lived in an elegant mansion in Kenwood and also owned a country estate in Charlevoix. Richard was their third son and eventually they had four. To help them bring up their family they decided, when Richard was five years old, to hire a governess.

The Loeb family had German ancestry but, unlike the Leopolds, weren't first-generation immigrants. Perhaps this influenced their choice of governess. Where Leopold was brought up by a series of European girls the Loebs settled on a Canadian, Emily Struthers. Both intellectual and strict, Struthers seems to have played a major part in shaping - though perhaps "distorting" would be a better word - Loeb's personality.

Loeb attended the Lab School, but Struthers gave him extra tuition at home. With this extra help and his natural intelligence he made rapid progress, and ended up skipping several grades; he graduated from University High School, a prep school with close ties to the University of Chicago, at the age of 13. This was a remarkable achievement academically but put him in a difficult position socially. He started at the university in the fall of 1919, still only 14 years old; most of his fellow students were 18 or older.

As well as pushing him on academically Struthers also exerted control over Loeb's private life. Her motive seems to have been to keep him away from distractions that would interfere with his studies, but both Leopold and Clarence Darrow later wondered if she had helped warp him into the killer he became. The young Loeb was discouraged from playing with boys his own age, and severe limits were placed on how he could enjoy himself. Detective novels were forbidden as frivolous, but Loeb developed a passion for them anyway. He read them in secret and began to build a fantasy life that involved crime. With a childhood friend, Jack Mengal, he started to break more serious rules; the two boys stole a vase from a neighbor's house.5 They played poker together and sometimes strip poker; at least once this ended with them wrestling naked on a bed. When he was accepted at university and started hanging out with his fellow students he and

Mengal drifted apart; the other boy later ended up in Pontiac Reformatory.

The household gradually became the battleground for a contest between Anna Loeb and Emily Struthers, with the prize being the affections of Richard. Loeb felt that his parents neglected him, although he thought they probably didn't mean to, and Struthers became ever more influential in his life. The relationship wasn't an easy one, though. Feeling pressured and restricted both by his parents and Struthers, Loeb started to lie about his activities. Sometimes this was about harmless things - saying he'd been studying in the library when really he'd been playing cards. Sometimes it wasn't.

When Loeb was nine his brother Thomas was born. This increased the tension in the household. Struthers resented the new arrival and intensified her attempts to influence Richard. Part of this involved further pressure on him to do well. Loeb was clever, but he was expected to be brilliant. Luckily for him Struthers' tutoring and his own intelligence let him get through school with high marks despite not working very hard. When he did have any trouble his popularity let him crib from the other boys. All this changed when he got to university, though. Being so young he found it difficult to relate to his fellow students, and Struthers couldn't help him as she had before. Although Loeb found a group to hang out with the age gap made things difficult. After his first year, though, another young student started at the university. It was the 15 year old Nathan Leopold.

[2]
UNIVERSITY

Leopold wasn't as far ahead of his peer group as Loeb was, but he still started university two months before his sixteenth birthday. He had already started to hang around with the small group that Loeb associated with, and stayed part of it after beginning his studies in the fall of 1920. At first relations between the two had been cool, and even hostile. Their personalities were very different, Loeb sociable and charming while Leopold was reserved and shy. Over time things thawed, though. There were more commonalities than differences. Both were much younger than the other students, and both were Jewish. They came from wealthy families who lived in the same neighborhood. Initial disdain soon thawed on both sides and by the time Leopold was admitted to university they were friends. The relationship was not an equal one though; the quieter Leopold was mesmerized by Loeb and constantly trying to monopolize his attention. It was an unhealthy situation that contributed greatly to what was to come.

As well as being unequal the relationship had also become sexual. As early as summer 1920 there was a physical element to their association, and they weren't very good at keeping it secret. A scandal that summer had later repercussions.

Leopold had been at the University of Chicago for a year when he and Loeb both moved to Ann Arbor and the University of Michigan. At first they shared a room, but after a few months Loeb joined the Zeta Beta Tau fraternity and moved into their house. One condition of his acceptance to the fraternity was that he end his friendship with Leopold; a fellow student who worked summers on the Charlevoix estate had started rumors of a homosexual relationship based on what he'd seen there in

1920. Eager for the social advantages of being in the fraternity Loeb agreed, and relations between him and Leopold cooled - outwardly, at least. They stopped being seen in public unless accompanied by others, but in secret they occasionally went drinking together. Loeb later said this was all on the advice of his brother Allen.

In 1922 Leopold transferred back to the University of Chicago and graduated Phi Beta Kappa in March 1923. Loeb stayed at Michigan. He lived in the Zeta Beta Tau fraternity house, but his frat brothers thought his behavior was often childish and he wasn't allowed to mentor pledges. He graduated in June, the youngest student to graduate in the history of the University of Michigan (although the university doesn't acknowledge this publicly.) Apart from that his academic career had nothing to distinguish it, but he planned to enter the law school at Chicago. Leopold, on the other hand, intended to tour Europe in summer 1924 - his father had already given him $3,000 for this - then go to Harvard Law School. They both decided to start law school in fall 1924, and in the meantime they studied part-time courses at University of Chicago. Free from the scrutiny of the fraternity they became inseparable friends again.6

Enter the Supermen

Both Leopold and Loeb were outstandingly intelligent, and although their personalities were very different they shared a number of traits. One of these was an almost incredible level of arrogance. Both of them seem to have believed themselves to be on a higher level than the "normal" people who surrounded them, and their feelings of superiority led them towards a philosophy that they thought described them perfectly. The identity they adopted was that of the Übermensch, the "ideal being" described by Friedrich Nietzsche.

Many politicians and others have claimed inspiration from the works of Nietzsche, but in many ways he was a vehemently anti-political thinker. Above all else Nietzsche was an individualist, and he despised those who followed an organized system of thought as lacking imagination and integrity. He disliked organized religion - especially Christianity, which he saw as being focused on "other-worldly" rewards at the expense of self-improvement in the real world - and had a complex view of morality. He also strongly criticized anti-Semitism, which was a powerful force in his native Germany and common in the USA of the 1920s.

Between 1883 and 1885 Nietzsche published the four volumes of Also Sprach Zarathustra, a philosophical novel that expanded his earlier idea of the Übermensch. Although Übermensch is often translated into English as superman the original German word is more nuanced and can also be translated as beyond human or over human. In the novel Nietzsche argued that "God is dead," in the sense that the concept of God could no longer be used as a source of values, and that Christianity's idea of an eternal soul devalues life and is destructive. In contrast the Übermensch unifies soul and body in a single entity and is focused on achievements in life. Nietzsche saw the Übermensch as devoting his or her energies to constructive goals, but it was an easy idea to misinterpret. For two young men as self-obsessed as Loeb and Leopold this philosophy, with its implications of superiority, was irresistible and they ran with it in an appalling direction. They decided that they could prove their status as Nietzschean supermen by committing the perfect crime.

[3]
THE SLIPPERY SLOPE

In fact Leopold and Loeb had already committed many crimes and had even attempted murder. The Loeb family had an estate in Charlevoix, Michigan, which the boys regularly visited. During a visit in the summer of 1920 they were caught in a compromising position by the student who had a summer job there, Hamlin Buchman. Outraged at what he saw as their perversion he wrote to Sam Leopold and Allen Loeb about what he had seen; worse from the boys' point of view, he also later wrote to the Zeta Beta Tau fraternity to urge them not to admit "a pair of cocksuckers." In the wealthy and influential circles their families moved in this threatened social disaster, and they moved quickly to limit the potential damage. Allen Loeb travelled to Charlevoix to help sort out the mess, and his intervention helped later when Loeb applied to the fraternity. He also advised his brother never to be seen alone with Leopold; they should always have a "chaperone" with them who could vouch for their behavior. The problem had been largely controlled, but this wasn't enough for Leopold and Loeb. They wanted to hit back at Buchman and ending their friendship with him wasn't enough; they wanted him dead.

Leopold said later that they had spent months searching for a foolproof way of killing Buchman. The problem was that they couldn't think of one that wouldn't leave them implicated in his death. Finally they had an idea. By staging an accident they hoped to eliminate Buchman without attracting any suspicion. Drowning is a common cause of death now, especially among adolescent males, and it was just as common in 1920. A water-related accidental death, then, was likely to be accepted as a tragic mishap. The method they decided on was to go out in a canoe with Buchman then capsize it and let him drown. They actually attempted this, but the plan failed; Buchman escaped death by swimming to shore.

The failure of this attempt didn't deter Leopold and Loeb from crime. Loeb spent much of his spare time playing cards, and by 1921 was regularly cheating. This didn't provide enough excitement, though, and he moved on to other crimes. Petty thefts provided some amusement at first, then vandalism was his next step; he began to throw bricks through car windshields and store windows. Leopold joined in, driven by a twisted pact he had made with Loeb.

Loeb's fantasy world placed him in the center as a popular, gifted and powerful figure, worshipped by others. Leopold's hero worship gave him the chance to experience the same feeling in real life. At the same time Loeb was worried that Leopold's constant desire for sex ran the risk of them being caught again. The solution came to be known as "the compact." Loeb would think of crimes and Leopold would help him commit them. In return they would arrange a date and time to have sex. This let

Loeb control the risks while also getting him a compliant partner for his misdemeanors. Leopold was also worried, but for a different reason - he was frightened of the consequences of the crimes they committed. The lure of sex with Loeb drove him on, though.

The crimes got worse. Cars were stolen. Prank phone calls turned to fake fire alarms and then to arson. In 1923 a friend of Loeb's went on holiday with his family. The two planned to burgle the house and they went prepared for violence. In their car they had ropes to tie up the maid and a pistol to kill the night watchman. Luckily the car broke down on the way and the plan came to nothing.7 Finally they took the fateful step of planning another attempt at murder.

The chain of events that led to this decision was a complex one. In November 1923 they planned to burgle two fraternity houses in Ann Arbor. One was the Delta fraternity that had led Leopold on then refused to pledge him; remembering the humiliation he wanted revenge. The other was Zeta Beta Tau, which had accepted Loeb. At first it seemed perfect; both would get revenge on the frats they hated and Leopold would get his perk for helping Loeb. When they set it in motion and drove back to Ann Arbor, though, a problem surfaced. It was one that had come up before, and was leading to increasing tension between them.

Their trip to Michigan took place on November 10, 1923.8 The break-in at Zeta Beta Tau was no problem. The takings were slim - they got away with $80 in cash, an Underwood portable typewriter and a handful of watches and penknives - but both of them had generous allowances and it wasn't really about the money anyway. When it came to the other robbery, though, Loeb started to get second thoughts. He didn't know the layout of the building and worried that this made the risks unacceptable. It wasn't the first time he'd backed out of a crime - he loved making plans but often held off from actually carrying them out - and as always it enraged Leopold. Part of this was that he saw his promised sexual reward disappear; another part might have been that he idolized Loeb and hated to have his illusions challenged. Either way he wasn't happy, and he badgered Loeb into going ahead with it. In the end they did break into the Delta frat house, but it was a half-hearted attempt and they only stole a camera.

In the car on the return journey Leopold let his frustration bubble over. The relationship was too one-sided, he said. He always agreed to join in whatever plan came up, but still Loeb kept his distance. The robbery he'd wanted had been a farce, and other cancelled crimes had denied him the rewards he craved. The lingering bitterness over the New Year incident spurred him on. It was going to take a lot for Loeb to smooth the waters this time.

Of course Loeb, with the charm Leopold could never resist, delivered. Calming Leopold by professing his loyalty and affection, he suggested that they cement their relationship more closely. Up to now nothing they had done had made it into the newspapers; some thefts and fires just weren't attention-grabbing enough. There wasn't much chance of the frat house burglaries changing that. There was one crime guaranteed to get a media reaction, though - murder. Loeb now proposed that they kidnap and murder a boy from a wealthy family; they could demand a ransom, which would be a huge challenge to collect without being caught, and the crime would be famous. It would be a bold and decisive act, and nobody would ever know who'd done it. Of course, one other aspect that Leopold might not think of was that it would give Loeb more control over him. He could never risk a secret like that being revealed. Far from making the relationship more equal Loeb's proposal would give him more power than ever.

Leopold didn't see the potential drawbacks, though, and threw himself into the plan. The intention was to confirm their role as Übermenschen by committing a crime that dull-witted, mundane people would never have the imagination or intellect to solve. The process of planning this perfect crime would increasingly occupy them for the next six months.

[4]
THE MURDER OF ROBERT FRANKS

The planning that went into the killing was elaborate in the extreme. The only automobile Leopold and Loeb could count on having access to was Leopold's red Willys Knight. A brightly colored sporty coupé, this was a conspicuous vehicle and they decided it was too risky to use it for the crime.9 Rather than steal a car an intricate plan was devised to rent one under a false name. In late April Leopold opened a bank account in the name of Morton D. Ballard, and Loeb registered at the Morrison hotel under the same name. Letters were sent to Ballard at the hotel, to begin building up an identity, and on May 9 Leopold went to a local Rent-a-Car office and introduced himself as Ballard. He claimed to be a salesman recently posted in from Peoria and asked to rent a car, offering a generous $400 deposit in lieu of the three references required by Rent-a-Car but which he couldn't provide. The hire office insisted on at least one reference, though, and "Ballard" named his friend Mr. Louis Mason. A phone call to "Mason" - Loeb, waiting by the pay phone at a nearby delicatessen - secured the reference, and Leopold collected the car. He and Loeb kept it for a few hours then handed it back, at which point Loeb returned to the Morrison. The old suitcase he'd brought when he checked in was missing. He quickly realized that the staff had noticed that his bed had not been slept in and become suspicious about his reservation. He immediately left the hotel; the room had served its purpose and Leopold had been accepted as a reliable customer by the hire office.

Leopold and Loeb hadn't chosen a specific victim but they had decided on a hunting ground. Their plan was to cruise the streets around the Harvard School after the pupils had been released and abduct a boy who was walking alone. There were obvious dangers in this, because the school was only a few blocks from both their homes and many people in the district knew them. The same factor also offered advantages, though, and the pair decided these could be exploited.

On May 20 they prepared the equipment they would need for the abduction and killing. They had decided to kill their victim by strangulation, with one of them pulling on each end of the ligature so they would be equally guilty. Loeb visited a hardware store on Cottage Grove Street and bought a length of rope to use for the killing. He then visited another hardware store further down Cottage Grove and bought a chisel. Rejoining Leopold, they next went to a drug store where Leopold tried to buy a bottle of hydrochloric acid. Failing, he tried again at another drugstore and this time was successful. The rest of the equipment was collected together at Leopold's house - rags to use as gags, a bottle of ether to keep the victim quiet and a pair of hip boots belonging to Leopold's brother. Leopold took a roll of zinc oxide tape from the bathroom and used it to bind the chisel's sharp blade; it could now be safely gripped and the wooden handle used as a bludgeon. A car cloak was added; it would be used to conceal the body in the back of the car. Finally they added some extra security. If anyone caught them in the act it would be necessary to silence them instantly. Chisels and gags might work on a schoolboy, but more would be needed if an adult came across them. Two automatic pistols went into the car with the rest of the equipment, a .45 for Loeb and a .380 for Leopold.

The final stage of the crime was to be a ransom demand. Leopold and Loeb planned to demand $10,000 for the safe return of their victim, and they carefully planned a method of collecting the money without risking themselves. Of course they never had any intention of honoring the deal; they were well aware that a released kidnap victim could identify them and that abducting a boy from their own neighborhood and old school was especially dangerous. The victim would be killed as soon as possible after the snatch, and the corpse concealed well enough that it wouldn't be found until after the money had been delivered. To speed up the ransom demand they had already composed a series of letters. These told the boy's father not to contact the police, then went on to describe the elaborate process for handing over the money. Because a specific victim hadn't been chosen the letters were generic; the victim's address would be printed on the envelope after the killing. Now Leopold typed up final copies of all the letters on the portable typewriter they'd stolen from Zeta Beta Tau.[10] They both knew that letters could be traced to the typewriter that had produced them by examining wear and imperfections on the keys, but being stolen there was nothing to link the Underwood to either of them. If the police did search Leopold's house they'd find the heavy Hammond office model in the library, and good luck tying the notes to that. The Underwood would be long gone by then.

The next day, with all their preparations made, Leopold got up early and went to college at eight o'clock as usual. Around eleven he met up with Loeb at the school. They stashed their equipment in the rented car and drove with both cars to Kramer's restaurant on 35th and Cottage. Arriving there about quarter past twelve they put up the side curtains on the rented car, then ate lunch. Around half past one they drove to Leopold's house, parked his car in the garage and masked the license plate of the green Willys-Knight.11 That looked a bit suspicious, but plates weren't as strictly regulated back then and it seemed less risky than having the number noted. By about quarter of two they were parked in Ingleside Avenue, a small street running parallel to Ellis Avenue where the Harvard School was located.

Now it became obvious that eagerness had got the better of them; they were too early. They had no chance of finding a victim until the school let out - three o'clock at the very least. In fact it was probably going to be later still because the boys often hung around in groups after school, chatting to friends or setting up a ball game on a nearby vacant lot. They'd need to hang out until the cliques started to break up and the boys began making their way home, and then they'd have to wait until one got far enough away from his friends that they could snatch him unobserved.

In fact hanging around the school for hours was almost insanely risky. It was within three blocks of both their homes - a single block over from Leopold's. The boys they were stalking were the sons of family friends, and if the attempt failed they might be recognized. Loeb's younger brother Tommy was a pupil there himself, and knew that he'd been cruising around the school that afternoon. By choosing a hunting ground where they were both quite well known they had made things much more dangerous for themselves. Maybe that was part of the thrill.

Loeb certainly didn't let the risk put him off. He walked from Ingleside over to the school, to reconnoiter the area. A group of boys were playing outside under the supervision of a tutor named James Seass. Loeb chatted to him for a while, all the time looking around for likely targets. The group included a boy they'd already discussed as a possible victim. Sol Levinson's son John ticked all the boxes. He was young enough to be easily overpowered and his wealthy family could pay the ransom. He knew Loeb, so it would be easy to get him into the car without a fuss. Now Loeb chatted to him about his baseball game for a while, then said goodbye to Seass and wandered round the front of the school. Out front he found his brother, and was talking to him when he heard a whistle from across the street. He looked up, and there was Leopold. Loeb crossed over and Leopold told him there was another group of boys playing on Ingleside that looked promising.

The two walked back to Ingleside and scouted out the group, but decided none of them would do. Next they headed down to Drexel Boulevard and 49th Street, where more boys were playing. Levinson had now joined this group, and they watched for a while then went back to the car. Drexel has a wide median strip, and they parked on the west side, opposite the vacant lot. Now they found a new problem - from that distance they couldn't recognize individual boys. Leopold had a solution for that though; they drove to his house and he picked up a pair of field glasses, while Loeb went to the drug store on 47th and Ellis. He bought two packs of gum and leafed through the phone book, finding Sol Levinson's address so they could guess John's route home from school.12

After picking up Leopold they drove back to the same spot on Drexel and watched the boys through the glasses for a while. John Levinson and a couple of others headed up an alley towards the school. They waited for him to come back, but he didn't. Wondering where he'd gone, Loeb looked for him in the alley. There was no sign of him. He wasn't playing outside his house when they drove past there, either. In fact Levinson had been collected by the family chauffeur and taken to a dental appointment. As much as everyone hates dentists, this visit had probably saved his life.

Loeb returned to the car and they drove off down Drexel, turned left then left again and headed back up Ellis. As they approached 48th

Street they saw a boy walking down the west side of the road. It was Bobby Franks.

Leopold pulled left onto 48th then turned the car around and drove back down Ellis. By the time that was done Franks was nearly at 49th Street. Loeb knew exactly where the boy lived - it was nearly opposite his own house. Franks was only two blocks from home and walking fast. There wasn't much time to get him. On the other hand, he explained to Leopold, he was the perfect victim. Small enough to be easily snatched, his father Jacob Franks doted on the boy and had made a fortune from his business activities. Starting as a pawnbroker, he'd made a clever investment in the Chicago gas company then gone on to be president of a watchmakers and a successful real estate broker. Nicknamed "Honest Jake" for his fairness, he was believed to be worth at least $4 million and maybe much more.13 He'd happily pay to get Bobby back.

There was a potential problem. Another boy was walking in the same direction not far behind Franks. They idled down the street, letting Franks open the gap, until they judged that the boys were far enough apart. Then they closed in.

Leopold pulled up close to Franks; Loeb opened the door and called, "Hey, Bob!" Franks stopped, and Loeb offered him a ride home. The boy declined, but Loeb then asked him to get in so they could talk about a tennis racket. Franks climbed into the car and Leopold set off along Ellis. Just over a block later he turned left onto 50th Street. Franks still suspected nothing, because Loeb had said they would drive round the block, but almost as soon as the car turned off Ellis the trap was sprung. Loeb grabbed him, clapped a hand across his mouth to silence him and hit him four times on the head with the handle of the chisel.14

Stunned, Franks slumped on his seat. The blows hadn't knocked him completely out, though, and he was moaning in pain. Frightened of being seen, Loeb hauled him into the back seat. To silence the boy's cries he stuffed a rag into his mouth then pushed him to the floor and covered him with the car cloak. Semiconscious and choking on the gag, the boy asphyxiated to death within minutes.

This hadn't been in the plan; rather than being strangled in a perverse bonding ritual Franks was now dead on the floor of the car. Worse, blood from the gashes in his scalp was leaking onto the carpet. The seats were already smeared. Even in the time before forensics really took off the danger was obvious. Leopold, confronted with the mess, started to panic and Loeb had to spend several minutes calming him down. "This is terrible. This is terrible," he said, only regaining equilibrium slowly. When his composure came back, though, it came back all the way. It was only quarter past five and the sun wouldn't set for nearly three hours; having killed Robert Franks they now had to kill time, so they would have darkness to dispose of the body. Driving out towards the Indiana state line Loeb began stripping Franks' corpse. Leopold turned off onto a dead end road and pulled over. The dead boy's shoes were hidden in a bush, and his belt concealed nearby. His pants and socks were also removed but kept in the car for later disposal. The pair then retraced their tracks back to the main road and drove around a while longer, waiting for dusk.15 They stopped once at a drug store and Leopold called his girlfriend, Susan Lourie, to cancel their date for that evening. At Calumet Boulevard and 132nd Street they stopped again at a sandwich stall and Leopold bought hot dogs and root beer, which they ate in the car. Another hour of cruising aimlessly and finally it was dark enough for their purposes.

Ten miles southeast of the murder scene, Wolf Lake straddles the Illinois-Indiana state line. A few hundred yards from its western shore is the Burnham Greenway, a paved recreational track popular with walkers and cyclists. The Greenway follows the line of an older track. In 1924 it was the Pennsylvania Railroad, and in stretches the modern road runs along the top of an old embankment. To stop this embankment causing flooding in the low, wet ground around the lake drainage culverts were built through it, and Leopold and Loeb had chosen one of these as the last resting place of their victim.

Parking the car about 300 yards from the culvert, they dragged Franks from the back seat and turned the car cloak into an improvised stretcher. Loeb took the head and Leopold the feet, and they carried it over to the railway line. There they laid the body down and finished stripping it. The clothes were bundled into the cloak along with the short pants and socks they'd removed earlier. Now Leopold uncorked the bottle of hydrochloric acid.

The killers had been concerned that the body might be found before they could collect the ransom money, which would obviously put an end to that part of their plan. Their fears were to prove justified, but instead of finding a more effective way of disposing of the victim they outsmarted themselves yet again. It would have been simple enough to tie the body in the cloak with a couple of large rocks and throw it in one of the area's many rivers, but having chosen the culvert and scouted it out days earlier they didn't want to change their plans. Instead they decided to disfigure the body enough to make it unrecognizable, and that was where the acid came in. A heavy splash of the caustic liquid started to eat away at Franks' face. That wasn't enough for Loeb, though. He had the idea that men could be identified by the shape of their penis - apparently he thought his brother Tommy had an unusually-shaped one - so more acid was poured on the body's genitals. Franks had an appendectomy scar; more acid. Then Leopold pulled on the hip boots he'd taken from his house and waded into the drainage ditch. Dragging Franks in after him he pushed it head first into the culvert while Loeb washed blood from his hands. The body had splashed when it hit the water, though, and his cold wet shirt and the smell of the acid distracted Leopold. Eager to get the job done he didn't push the corpse in far enough and one foot remained visible. That mistake was bad enough. What followed was worse.

    Leopold had taken off his coat and shoes before donning the boots and getting into the water. Now he climbed the embankment; it was darker down by the culvert and he was having trouble tying his shoelaces. "Hey, Dick, can you get my coat?" he called.

"Sure, Babe." Loeb shook the water from his hands and picked up the old coat. Something slipped from the pocket and hit the ground; the water flowing in the culvert masked any noise it made. Loeb bundled the rest of the boy's clothing into the cloak and started up the embankment towards his friend. In the darkness a stocking slipped out of the bundle and fell unnoticed to the grass. That didn't really matter, of course; it belonged to Franks, not one of the killers, and at that time the police wouldn't have got any forensic data from it. They'd still made a fatal mistake though.

Walking back towards the car, Leopold never thought to check his pockets. He and Loeb had set out to commit the "perfect crime," but in fact they had bungled it. Before they even moved on to the next stage - the ransom demand - their detection was already almost inevitable.

[5]
CLEANING UP

On November 19, 1904 Nathan Freudenthal Leopold, Junior was born in Chicago to a wealthy family of German immigrants. As was normal among the children of the very rich at the time his parents played a small part in his childhood, and much of his upbringing was left to a series of nurses and governesses. The traditionalist Leopold family favored European girls for these positions, and the young Leopold and his brothers Samuel and Foreman were raised in an environment where German was routinely spoken. Leopold's first words, spoken at the age of only four months, were "Nein, nein. Mama." His nurse at the time, and for the first five years of his life, was Marie Giessler, known as Mimie.

Leopold and Loeb had carefully worked out how to get rid of the physical evidence. Thanks to the blood there was a lot more than they'd bargained on, but they went ahead with the cleanup anyway. On the way back to the city they stopped so Leopold could call home. He told his father that he'd be slightly late and that his aunt, who he'd arranged to drive home, should wait for him. He didn't go directly home, though. First they headed for Loeb's house. Bobby Franks' clothes went into the furnace. They wanted to burn the cloak, too, but decided not to. It was too large and they were worried it would create a smell throughout the house. They stashed it under some bushes in the garden for later disposal. Next they got a bucket of water and some cloths and tried to clean up the blood in the car. It was dark and they were in a hurry, so they didn't make a very good job, but they planned to finish it next day. Only then did they drive to

Leopold's house, dump the hire car just up the street and go inside.

Leopold took his aunt home while Loeb chatted to his father. Leopold was away slightly longer than his father might have expected, because he'd stopped to make a phone call telling the shocked Mrs Franks that her son had been kidnapped. When he returned he said goodnight to his father then played cards with Loeb for a while, "for fun" as he clarified later. Finally, just before 1:30, he drove Loeb the three blocks to his house. On the way Loeb realized the murder weapon was still in his coat pocket.

# # #

The Kenwood district of Chicago was wealthy, and sometimes attracted burglars. The Chicago police department patrolled it regularly enough, but some residents weren't reassured and took extra precautions. That included hiring night watchmen. The watchman's job suited Bernard Hunt. He lived in a small white clapboard house three miles away on South Aberdeen, and patrolling these elegant mansions paid his bills with enough to spare. It was quiet, too. Kenwood's wealthy might worry about break-ins, but nothing really happened here. There had been a few minor fires and some vandalism last year, but nothing much since. Rich kids acting up, he supposed.

That's what he thought at 1:30 in the morning of May 22, when the flashy sports car came round the corner of 49th and Greenwood and something spun from the window. Whatever it was hit the street and bounced nearly to the sidewalk. As the car swept past Hunt got a good look at it. Yes, rich kids all right; he couldn't tell the color so well under the orange streetlamps, but it had disk wheels, custom reflectors and a fancy light-colored top. Curious, he crossed the street and looked round for whatever had been thrown. Soon he found it; a chisel, with thick white tape wrapped round the blade. He picked it up. That was a strange thing to do to a good tool. And why had it been ditched? He examined it more closely, and saw the dark crusts on the handle and smeared into the tape. That looked like dried blood. Frowning, he pocketed it and returned to his beat.

The chisel was still weighing on his mind an hour later, when a black Essex sedan came rattling its way up the street. The hand-cranked bell on the passenger door marked it as a police car even before he could make out the white star and lettering beside it, and he walked to the curb and stuck a hand out. The Essex juddered to a halt beside him and the side curtain, buttoned against the cool night, was pulled open. Inside he recognized Officers Enos and Milligan of the "flivver squad" - the new team set up to patrol the city in cars.16 Kenwood was part of their regular beat and they'd stopped to chat with him several times.

"Hey, Bernie, what's up?" asked Enos. Hunt reached for his pocket.

"This got thrown out a car about an hour ago," he said, handing over the chisel. "Looks like blood on the handle there. Thought you better see it."

Enos turned the tool in his hands, thinking for a moment. "Reckon you're right too. Did you get a look at the car?"

Hunt nodded. "I saw it."

"OK then, jump in. We'll head over to the station and get a statement. Best to have it on paper if it turns out somebody got smacked on the head with this."

# # #

Tony Minke, an immigrant from Poland, worked for the Pennsylvania Railroad as a maintenance worker. His job took him along the company's tracks, looking for anything that could be a problem. It wasn't the best-paid job in the world, but it was an important one. It didn't take much to cause a train wreck. Just last September 30 people had died in Wyoming on the Chicago, Burlington and Quincey Railroad when a bridge washed out after heavy rain. In this low, wet ground a lot of track was raised on embankments, and these relied on culverts for drainage. Flooding along the embankment could cause rapid erosion, and even slight settling of the tracks might be enough to send a train off the line. Tony Minke wanted to work his way up in this new country and he was determined to do his job well. No flood was going to happen on his stretch of line if he could do anything about it.

On the morning of May 22 he was checking the track along the Wolf Lake section of the line, looking for debris that could block a culvert. Passing one culvert he glanced down the embankment and saw something white protruding from the narrow tunnel. At first thinking it might be a piece of trash stuck in the culvert mouth he scrambled down to look. As he came closer he realized, to his horror, that it was a human foot. A small human foot.

Minke climbed down and looked inside. The small cadaver was stuffed grotesquely into the culvert, and even in the shadowed pipe he could see that the face and body were revoltingly burned. He looked along the track for his colleague. "Paul! Get over here, quick!"

Paul Korff heard the urgency in Minke's voice and ran along the line. "What ya got, Tony?"

"There's a dead child in here, a boy. I think he's been murdered."

Korff looked into the pipe. "Think so too. Hell, we better get the cops out here." He stood up and backed away, repelled by the sight. Then a tiny glint of light caught his eye.

He looked down. A pair of horn-rimmed glasses lay in the rough grass.

[6]
Errors, Suspicions, and Arrests

Despite the years of build-up and the intricate planning that had gone into the crime, the deception plan developed by Leopold and Loeb began to unravel within hours of Franks' death. Perhaps rattled by the unexpected problems during the actual killing they made a series of errors from that point on. The complicated plan now started to work against them, as there were too many opportunities for people to remember them and too many things to go wrong. They hadn't yet realized their mistakes, though, and kept on with their scheme.

Next day Leopold picked Loeb up around 11:30 and they moved the rental car to Leopold's garage. While they were scrubbing the rest of the blood from the seats and carpet Sven Englund, the chauffeur, came in and asked him what they were doing. Leopold told him that they had spilled some red wine in the car and he didn't want his father to know. Englund offered to help them clean it, but they declined. They kept scrubbing until the stains were as faint as they could get them, then set out to get the money.

Like everything else about the crime the system for collecting the ransom was carefully planned and complex. The main concerns were to avoid being seen at any stage, and to eliminate opportunities for the police to ambush them. This was the hardest part of the plan, and Loeb was delighted at the ingenious solution they came up with. The first stage had been the phone call to the Franks telling him that their son had been kidnapped. Next a special delivery letter was mailed, containing the ransom note. Another phone call was made to the Franks' home the next day with further instructions; Franks was to get in a cab that would come to his house, and would be taken to a trash can on a street corner. Taped to the trash can would be a note directing him to go a drug store and wait. A phone call to the drug store would then tell him to get on a train leaving in a few minutes from a nearby station - the idea being that he wouldn't have time to tell the police what was planned - and go to the telegraph message box in the last car. In the message box would be a final note telling him to go out on the back platform and wait for the train to pass a distinctive brick factory. On passing this he was to count to five then throw the parcel of money as far from the track as he could. Leopold and Loeb would be waiting nearby in the hire car, watching for the parcel to be thrown. Because Franks wouldn't know what to do with the money until he boarded the train it would be impossible for him to tell the police where the drop-off was; even if police had managed to board the train with him they wouldn't be able to do anything. If the train slowed or stopped, on the other hand, they simply wouldn't collect the money. The plan seemed foolproof.

It wasn't, though. They couldn't get the envelope to stick to the trashcan, so that cutout was abandoned and they decided to send Franks directly to the drug store. Loeb, disguised in a pair of glasses and an overcoat and hat belonging to his father, bought a ticket to Michigan City from Illinois Central Station and boarded the train at 2:30, half an hour before it left. He concealed the final note in the Car 507 message box then got off the train. Outside he rejoined Leopold, who'd been making phone calls. First he called the Yellow Cab Company to order a car for Jacob Franks. Next he phoned Franks himself, and told him to go to the Bogart de Ross drug store on East 63rd and wait there for a call. Franks stalled. He said that something had come up and he needed more time. Leopold insisted; Franks needed to go right now. Then he hung up. When Loeb came out the station they drove to the Walgreens on 67th and Stony Island, and stationed themselves by the pay phone.

The cab arrived at the Franks house as arranged, but Leopold hadn't told the driver where to go and Jacob Franks couldn't remember. That didn't matter though. Franks hadn't just been stalling after all; something had come up. A lucky journalist had heard rumors of a child kidnapping involving the Franks. Then he heard a boy's body had been found out by Wolf Lake. He put the two together and called Jacob Franks, who dispatched his brother-in-law to check it out. When Leopold called Franks had just been told that his brother-in-law had positively identified the body as his younger son. There would be no attempt to pay the ransom, and the police were already searching for the killer of Bobby Franks.

To pass the time as they waited to call they bought a paper from a newsstand. On the front page was a story about the corpse of an unidentified boy found near 121st and Railroad Avenue, out near Wolf Lake. Seeing this, Loeb wanted to ditch the plan and start covering their tracks. Leopold argued, though. Sure, the corpse was found. It couldn't be identified, though, because they'd stripped off the clothing with its identifying marks and burned away the face with acid. There was still time to get the money from the Franks before they knew it was their son in the culvert. What drove Leopold on at this point isn't known. It wasn't for need of the money; he got enough from his family already. Maybe he feared that if they backed out Loeb would again deny him the sex he needed. Maybe he wanted to show how clever his ransom plan was, by getting the cash even when so much had gone wrong. Either way he talked Loeb round.

Leopold called the Bogart de Ross store from Walgreens, but the clerk told him there was no Mr. Franks in the building. They moved up the street to another drug store and waited ten minutes,[17] then called again. Still no Mr. Franks. That did it. Now suspecting that the body had already been identified they abandoned the ransom plan and returned the hire car. Most of the evidence had already been disposed of - they thought - and now they just had to get rid of the cloak and typewriter then wait for the fuss to die down. They'd worked out a story for their movements the day before and if either was questioned they could name the other and get them to back it up. They didn't have anyone else who could confirm it for them but it should be enough. They agreed that this alibi would be used for the next week; if anything happened after that they would simply say they couldn't remember what they'd done that day.

# # #

On the evening of Saturday May 24 Leopold and Loeb went on a double date with Susan Lurie and Lorraine Nathan. At about ten they dropped the girls home then returned to their own houses. At two in the morning they sneaked out and met up at a restaurant on 51st Street. With them they had the Underwood typewriter and the bloodstained car cloak. Leaving the restaurant, they drove southeast in Leopold's car while Loeb went to work on the typewriter. He snapped off the key tips that made each typewriter unique. Leopold drove to Jackson Park Lagoon, where Loeb threw the keys from one bridge and the typewriter off another. He lugged a can of gasoline from the trunk, dumped the cloak on the shore and saturated it with fuel. A match took care of the rest.18

With the last evidence disposed of they returned home. Tired by the long night, Leopold was still in bed next morning when his father shook him awake with some bad news. There were two police officers downstairs and they wanted to speak to him.

In fact they wanted more than that. Leopold was taken to the State Attorney's office and asked to make a statement. He did, explaining that he was familiar with Hegewisch Swamp through his well-known bird watching activities. The police asked him who else in his class went out to the swamp and he obliged, giving them a list of names. Leopold was confident the police were satisfied with his explanations. At this point he was barely a suspect anyway; the police had only wanted to speak to him because the game warden had named him as someone who often travelled to the area where the body was found, and they hoped he would be able to name others who frequented the area.

There were suspects, of course. The ransom note received by the Franks had clearly been written by an educated man - quite unusual in criminals - and three teachers at the school had quickly been arrested. One was held only briefly then released, but two more were still in custody when Leopold was first interviewed. One reason for the interview was that the police were hoping Leopold would name one of the teachers as someone who went to the swamps. More pieces of the puzzle were starting to fall into place, though, and gradually Leopold began to stand out more clearly from the sea of potential killers.

The glasses had continued to interest the police. Leopold had denied having lost his glasses and was confident they would be impossible to identify as his. The prescription for the lenses was a common one and there was nothing remarkable about the frames. The only unusual thing about the glasses were the hinges on the earpieces. These were manufactured in New York and there was only one optician in Chicago that sold them. Once the hinges had been identified the optician was swiftly tracked down, and police visited Almer Coe to ask him how many pairs of glasses with that hinge design he had sold. There were only three. One of the customers was a woman, named Marie; when the police visited her at work she didn't have them with her, but was able to take the police to her home and show them the glasses.[19] Another was prominent local attorney Jerome Frank, who the police immediately ruled out because he was on a tour of Europe. The third was Nathan Leopold.

On May 29 Leopold was picked up again and taken to the LaSalle Hotel, where State's Attorney Robert Crowe had taken a room.[20] Confronted with the new evidence about the glasses, he said they must have fallen from his pocket when he tripped while trying to photograph a rare bird. Assistant State's Attorney Joseph Savage handed him the glasses and asked him to demonstrate. Leopold repeatedly tripped himself and fell to the floor, but the glasses stayed firmly in his pocket.

Suspicion was now falling directly on Leopold. He stalled for as long as possible but eventually decided that, even though more than a week had passed, it was time to deploy the alibi. He told his interrogators that on May 21 he'd met Loeb and they had gone driving. They'd headed over to Marshall Fields and had lunch at a grill room. After that they'd gone to Lincoln Park for the afternoon. Finally they'd picked up two girls named Mae and Edna - they hadn't learned their last names - and driven around with them for a while. When they couldn't persuade the girls to "come across" they dropped them off near a golf course and went for dinner at the Coconut Grove. The alibi covered Leopold's tracks for the whole day, but it didn't have a lot of evidence to back it up. It also pointed the investigation at Loeb. He was soon picked up and brought in to confirm the alibi. To avoid collusion he was questioned separately from Leopold and things started going wrong immediately. Knowing that the time limit on their alibi had passed, Loeb said that he didn't remember where he'd been that day. Leopold worked this out quickly; he believed that if the alibi had been confirmed he would have been released, so the fact he was still being held meant that Loeb wasn't talking. The problem was he couldn't communicate with Loeb - or not directly, at least. Watching for an opportunity he managed to get a journalist to unwittingly act as go-between. At Leopold's urging the reporter asked Loeb to "tell the truth about the two girls. Tell the police what you did with them. You can't get in any worse trouble than you are now. He said you'd understand."21 Realizing that Leopold had given the police the alibi, Loeb now "remembered" where he'd been eight days before and backed up Leopold's story.

It was too late, though. Evidence was piling up, and while the alibi might have been enough to deflect a casual inquiry it wasn't solid enough to withstand closer scrutiny. There were no independent witnesses who could confirm where they'd been during the critical time. The Coconut Grove wouldn't remember them eating there. Loeb had talked to people near the Harvard School during the afternoon, when they'd supposedly been at Lincoln Park. Instead of freeing them, as Leopold had expected, the police just noted the alibi and the questions kept coming.

The ransom note was also being analyzed, and the shape of the letters showed it had been typed on an Underwood portable. Detectives asked Leopold if he owned one; he said no. Next they searched his house but of course found nothing. At least they didn't find a portable typewriter. They did find Elizabeth Sattler, the maid, and asked her if she'd seen one around. She said she had; it had been in the house for three or four months, but she hadn't seen it the last couple of days.22

Without the typewriter, Leopold thought the police would be unable to get a match to the characters in the ransom note. Yet again his flawed genius let him down, though. He'd led a study group, which had typed up notes. Two journalists from the Chicago Daily News, Al Goldstein and Jim Mulroy, were interviewing friends of the boys. They found out about the study group from Arnold Maremont. Maremont told them that the notes were usually typed on an office typewriter but one time Leopold had used a portable. Did he have any notes from that session? Sure he did. Goldstein and Mulroy took them to the Royal typewriter company's local expert, H.P. Sutton, along with a copy of the ransom note. Sutton said they came from the same machine. That didn't quite pin Leopold directly to the note, but it was getting very close. Then on May 30 Sven Englund, the chauffeur, turned up at the State's Attorney's office. He had some information for the police that he thought might prove the boys' innocence. Instead he blew their alibis to pieces.

Crowe brought Loeb in for another interview and went over the alibi again. Point by point he talked through their movements on the fatal day. Had they gone out around eleven? Yes. Had they had lunch at the grill in Marshall's Field? Yes. Had they gone to Lincoln Park? Yes. Then he set up the killer blow. Had all their driving been done in Leopold's red Willys-Knight? Yes.

Crowe pounced. Englund had told him that he'd been fixing the coupe's brakes that day and the boys had driven off in a greenish or gray car. They'd lied about the red one. From one of them that might just about have been an honest mistake, but from both it showed deliberate deception. What else were they lying about? Loeb denied it, insisting that Englund was either lying or mistaken, but the game was up.

In fact there was far more evidence against them than Loeb could even begin to imagine and the police were getting their hands on it fast. The Morrison Hotel's house detective had opened the suitcase left there by "Morton D. Ballard" and found four books from the University of Chicago library. Tucked inside one of them was a library card in the name of Richard Loeb.

The alibi was collapsing and Loeb could see the writing on the wall. He quickly worked out that his only chance of leniency was to confess all and blame as much on Leopold as he could. Stunned investigators listened as he calmly went through the planning of the crime and how it had been executed. They were getting a carefully edited version, though; some of the details were different from what they'd hear later. The plan had been Leopold's, he told them, and the aim had been excitement and money. Planning had started about two months ago. During the actual abduction and killing Loeb had been driving, and Leopold had struck the blows against Franks then gagged him. He also said that the plan had been to kill Franks with ether, and Leopold had suggested this because he had experience at etherizing birds for his collection.

There were holes in Loeb's story, though. He claimed to have been the driver right up to the point where they'd stopped for hot dogs, but couldn't remember the route they'd taken. He'd been following Leopold's directions, he said. He also told the interviewers that through the trip he'd kept checking Franks to see if he was moving, but that would have been difficult from the driver's seat. It didn't matter. Everything was going to come out soon enough.

[7]
Overwhelmed By Evidence

Even without the confessions the case against Leopold and Loeb was now solid. They'd thought their plan would put them beyond suspicion; instead all it had done was create dozens of chances for the police to confirm pieces of the jigsaw. The list of people who recognized them was growing by the day. The state had no shortage of witnesses to choose from:

- Charles E. Ward at the Hyde Park State Bank recognized Leopold as the customer calling himself "Morton D. Ballard."

- Arthur J. Doherty at the same bank recognized Loeb as having cashed a check for $100 signed by "Ballard."
- David Barish and Max Tucherman of Barish's Delicatessen recognized Loeb as having been there on May 9 and answering the phone when it rang; this was when Loeb, as "Louis Mason," vouched for "Ballard."
- William Herndon and Margaret Fitzpatrick of the Rent-A-Car Company recognized Leopold as "Morton D. Ballard."
- Lucille Smith and her daughter had been walking up 118th, not far from the culvert, at about 9:30 p.m. on May 21 when a car passed them. From photos they identified it as similar to a Willys-Knight tourer.
- Bernard Hunt, the night watchman, identified Leopold's Willys-Knight coupé as similar to the car the chisel was thrown from.

Having confessed, Leopold and Loeb were now willing to help turn up more vital evidence.

The police took them to Jackson Park Lagoon, and Loeb showed them where he'd sunk the typewriter and pointed out the partly burned robe. Then they went out to the Indiana state line, where Loeb found the belt he'd hidden. The stores where the rope, chisel and acid had been bought were visited, and the proprietors remembered selling them to customers answering the boys' descriptions. The Pullman car where Loeb had hidden the note to Jacob Franks was traced to a yard in New York City and the letter retrieved. A diver salvaged the typewriter from the lagoon and its serial number was traced; it was the one stolen in the Zeta Beta Tau burglary.

They'd told their story and, while they disagreed about who had struck the fatal blows, the rest of it could be solidly confirmed by physical evidence and witnesses. They had also been chatting freely with the press, not seeming to care that they were trashing any possible defense. "Why, we even rehearsed the kidnapping at least three times, carrying it through in all details, lacking only the boy we were to kidnap and kill," said Leopold, "It was just an experiment. It was as easy for us to justify as an entomologist in impaling a beetle on a pin." Loeb was even more arrogant: "This thing will be the making of me. I'll spend a few years in jail and I'll be released. I'll come out to a new life."23 There was no going back now.

On June 5, 1924 a grand jury indicted them both for murder and kidnapping. State's Attorney Crowe was already anticipating the likely defense, because he knew who had been hired to defend the killers and didn't underestimate the challenge that posed. Lawyers, psychiatrists and journalists were assembling for the case and Crowe wanted to nail it down firmly. He was confident, though. "We have the most conclusive evidence I've ever seen in a criminal case," he announced the day after the confessions were signed.24 The defense knew that too.

[8]
THE TRIAL OF THE CENTURY

The verdict of the trial was already a foregone conclusion; even without the confessions there was plenty of physical evidence to link Leopold and Loeb to Franks' death. The best they could hope for was to escape the rope, and it was obvious that even this would require a defense verging on genius. With two wealthy families involved, though, there were few limits to the legal representation they could afford. They were looking for a popular lawyer with a talent for defending seemingly hopeless cases. They chose Clarence Darrow.

The 67-year-old Darrow had an impressive but sometimes controversial reputation. Although he was born in Ohio his family had New England roots, and his father Amirus was an outspoken abolitionist before the Civil War. He was also a well-known religious freethinker, who was nicknamed "the village infidel." Darrow's mother Emily was also politically aware, one of the earliest supporters of women's rights and female suffrage. Darrow himself attended Allegheny College, a private liberal arts school in Pennsylvania, and then moved to the law school at the University of Michigan. He didn't graduate from either school, but was still admitted to the Ohio bar in 1878. He soon got involved in Democratic Party politics, which suited his radical family traditions. In 1887 he moved to Chicago, where he worked for city hall and became a frequent speaker at Democratic rallies and other political events. In 1893 he helped persuade the governor of Illinois to pardon three anarchists who had been jailed for the 1886 Haymarket bombing.

Darrow next tried corporate law, working for the Chicago & Northwestern Railway Company. This didn't suit him, though, and in 1894 he resigned to represent rail union leader Eugene V. Debs, who was on trial for leading the Pullman strike. Debs was acquitted in his first trial but later jailed in a second. This didn't stop Darrow developing a taste for defense work and later that year he represented Patrick Prendergast, an Irish political activist who had shot and killed Chicago mayor Carter Harrison, Sr.25 Prendergast's first attorney had tried and failed to have him found insane - which he probably was - and Darrow managed to get a hearing to appeal this ruling. He failed too, and Prendergast was hanged on July 14, 1894.

Whether or not Prendergast's fate influenced his views or not is unknown, but by 1924 Darrow was known as a staunch opponent of the death penalty. Given the disgust their crime had caused Leopold and Loeb were ideal candidates for the rope. Darrow knew that an acquittal was unrealistic. Most people would expect him to try for a verdict of not guilty by reason of insanity, but he knew the risks of that approach. As soon as he tried to argue that his clients were insane the prosecution would produce a string of experts to testify that they were not. He also wanted to avoid a trial by jury; given public opinion that would almost certainly result in the death penalty.

This was a difficult trial for Darrow in many ways. He had made his reputation defending the poor and disadvantaged, but now his clients were two offspring of the elite. He was called a hypocrite; the Leopold and Loeb families were accused of using their wealth to shield their sons from the consequences of what they'd done. Whipped up by the press, people jeered that Darrow had sold out to the rich for a million dollars. To counter the accusations he helped the families prepare a statement that there would be no large sums spent on lawyers or medical experts.26

Darrow later suggested $200,000 as a suitable fee and ended up with $65,00027 - which came to $30,000 after taxes - but he really wasn't in this for the money. What he wanted was a chance to get a hearing for his views on the death penalty, and with the attention this case was generating in the USA and worldwide it was the perfect opportunity. When Loeb's uncle Jacob got him out of bed late on May 31 he didn't hesitate to take the case. Between the grand jury and the start of the trial he had over six weeks to work out his strategy, and he used it well.

#   #   #

The trial opened in Chicago's Criminal Court on July 21, 1924. Judge John R. Caverley was presiding and Darrow wanted him firmly in charge of the proceedings. At 63 years old and close to retirement, the scholarly Caverley wasn't out to make a name for himself. Darrow felt that he could possibly be talked into sparing Leopold and Loeb's lives, but a jury would want them hanged. The key, then, was keeping their fate out of the hands of a jury and Darrow knew how that could be done.

In front of over 300 spectators - 200 of them members of the press - the elderly lawyer approached the bench. He quietly told the court that he would not try to have the trial moved, nor to stop the prosecution separating the kidnapping and murder charges. Crowe looked on suspiciously. Combining the charges was the obvious thing to do; that way, if Crowe failed to get a death sentence Darrow had won. On the other hand, with the charges separated Crowe had two chances. If the jury opted for life imprisonment on the murder indictments he could try to hang them for kidnapping. Then Darrow dropped his bombshell:

"We want to state frankly here that no one in this case believes that these defendants should be released or are competent to be. We believe that they should be permanently isolated from society... After long reflection and thorough discussion, we have determined to make a motion in this court for each of the defendants in each of the cases to withdraw our pleas of not guilty and enter a plea of guilty."28

Darrow had planned this well in advance and discussed it with the Leopold and Loeb families. He hadn't told the boys until that morning, though; he couldn't risk word leaking out, and with their habit of boasting it was too likely that it would. Now they were pleading guilty to both charges and Crowe had no chance to withdraw one of them and keep it in reserve.

Now Caverley called the defendants forward for questioning. He reminded them that as they had pled guilty he could now sentence them to death, and the minimum sentence would be at least 14 years in prison; with that in mind, did they still want to plead guilty? "Yes," they both answered. The trial was now, technically, a sentencing hearing, because guilt did not need to be established. More importantly for Darrow, if the boys were to hang it wouldn't be a decision shared between twelve men on a jury. Caverley would have to make it alone.

The main point of the hearing now was to identify aggravating or mitigating factors that might affect the sentence. Crowe led off, stating that Leopold and Loeb were privileged young men who had everything they could want but had turned to crime anyway. He painted the ransom as an important element, implying that the boys wanted it to pay gambling debts. His statement lasted an hour and at the end of it he told the court that he was going to press for the death penalty. Darrow responded; he simply said that there was no precedent for hanging two boys of that age and it would achieve nothing.29

Now Crowe started bringing forward the prosecution witnesses, to establish the brutality of the crime. As well as those who had seen the defendants as they put their plan into effect he also had testimony from three psychiatrists, then known as alienists, that they were sane and capable of understanding their actions. Darrow and his colleagues on the defense team, brothers Benjamin and Walter Bachrach, did almost no cross-examination; bringing out more details would only help Crowe's case. The State's Attorney kept stacking up the evidence for a week. There was plenty of it; by the end he had called 81 witnesses and proven beyond any shadow of a doubt that Leopold and Loeb were guilty. Of course that wasn't in doubt; they had already entered guilty pleas and Darrow had said he wouldn't contest any aspect of the case. Crowe insisted on his parade of witnesses, though. Later several commentators speculated that he'd harmed his case by doing so - certainly

Judge Caverley had looked irritated more than once.

Now it was Darrow's turn. Walter Bacharach had gone to the American Psychiatry Association's annual convention and hired its president - Dr. William A. White - and two other top members, Drs. William Healy and Bernard Glueck. Crowe's alienists were traditionalists who mainly looked for external symptoms of mental illness; Bacharach's followed the then-new teachings of Sigmund Freud and were more concerned with subconscious influences and motivations.30 Two more psychiatrists, Drs. Harold Hurlbert and Carl Bowman, also joined the defense team. For the rest of the hearing most of the excitement came from watching rival teams of doctors bitterly attack each other's competence, credibility and finally honesty.

As soon as Darrow introduced his first witness, Dr. White, Crowe objected. The only reason to call a psychiatrist, he argued, was to prove a defendant not guilty by reason of insanity. Because Leopold and Loeb had already admitted their guilt White's testimony would be "incompetent, irrelevant and immaterial."31 Judge Caverley disagreed and after several days of legal arguments White took the stand, followed by the others. Crowe objected constantly but the doctors went on. They all painted a dreadful picture.

Loeb, the doctors said, had been handicapped by Emily Struthers' strict upbringing. He had been placed under too much pressure and her constant punishments had taught him to lie. He was sexually repressed and believed himself less potent than his friends. All his life, said White, he had been heading for self-destruction.32 The other Freudians had varying opinions of Loeb, but all found him shallow, manipulative and deficient in normal emotions. Glueck, to whom Loeb admitted killing Bobby Franks, said he showed no remorse or regrets.

The doctors picked up on the fact that Leopold had trouble making friends, especially with women. He was traumatized by his mother's death and had submerged his physical inferiority in fantasies. Healy was shocked by his callousness when talking about the murder and diagnosed a paranoid personality. Glueck was struck by how strongly Leopold identified with the Nietzschean superman.

The testimony of these experts impressed Caverley. The crime had been dreadful but, the doctors said, it had happened because two abnormal personalities had been brought together. Finally Darrow himself took the stand to sum up for the defense. His two-day speech is reckoned to be the finest of his career and it drove home the points that had been made throughout the hearing. The packed courtroom and the hundreds of people outside clamoring to get in reinforced, as one reporter said, Darrow's argument that "the court was the only thing standing between the boys and a bloodthirsty mob."33

In his marathon speech Darrow discussed the roots of the crime in society, in the carnage of the Great War and in the mental abnormalities of the defendants. He scorned Crowe's claim that it was a robbery to pay off gambling debts; the debts in question amounted to $90 and were from one boy to the other - and they each had over $3,000 in the bank at the time. The boys, Darrow argued, were pawns of Nature and it would be wrong to kill such helpless creatures. The death penalty itself came under sustained fire; "If the state in which I live is not kinder, more humane, and more considerate than the mad act of these two boys, I am sorry I have lived so long."

He turned to the question of the guilty pleas. In the last ten years, he said, 450 people had pleaded guilty to murder in the city of Chicago and only one of them had been hanged (the judge then had been Crowe.)34 There had never been a case in Chicago where a boy under 21 (the age of majority at the time) had been hanged after a guilty plea.

It might, Darrow suggested, be a mercy for Leopold and Loeb to hang them. It wouldn't be a mercy for their innocent families, though, or the state of society. Finally he apologized for the time he had taken, and closed with a call for a more humane nation:

"If I can succeed, my greatest reward and my greatest hope will be that I have done something for the tens of thousands of other boys, for the countless unfortunates who must tread the same road in blind childhood that these boys have trod; that I have done something to help human understanding, to temper justice with mercy, to overcome hate with love."

He needn't have apologized for the length of his speech. Crowe's closing for the prosecution also took two days, much of which he spent attacking Darrow and the defense's psychiatrists.

Finally, on September 11, 1924, Judge Caverley brought the court to order for the last time. The boys couldn't be shown to be insane, he said, but then they weren't normal either; if they were the crime could not have happened. It would be easy to hang them. On the other hand they were young, and for that reason and because of their personalities life imprisonment might be a more severe punishment. For the good of society, though, neither of them could ever be free again. He had made his decision.

For the murder of Bobby Franks, Caverley said, Nathan Leopold and Richard Loeb should be confined at Joliet Prison for the rest of their natural lives. For the kidnapping, 99 years in Joliet. Sentence passed, Caverley checked himself and his wife into hospital to recover from the strain. When he came out he arranged to deal with nothing but divorce cases for the rest of his career.

[9]
PRISON

Even without the confessions the case against Leopold and Loeb was now solid. They'd thought their plan would put them beyond suspicion; instead all it had done was create dozens of chances for the police to confirm pieces of the jigsaw. The list of people who recognized them was growing by the day. The state had no shortage of witnesses to choose from:

After the trial Leopold and Loeb were incarcerated at Joliet Prison. In 1930 Loeb was transferred to the new prison at Statesville, and Leopold - who'd already been there for a spell in 1925 - managed a permanent transfer the next year. Prison staff initially tried to keep them separate but eventually relented and let them associate freely. They got involved in the prison school, where they taught classes to fellow inmates. When they arrived at Statesville the school only taught classes up to eighth grade, which was a big step up for many of the almost illiterate inmates but fell short of what the intellectual killers thought possible.

There was a problem, though, thanks to the prison system. Inmates had jobs within the prison, and could earn extra privileges from them. To attend the school they had to give up their jobs and associated perks, and few were willing to do that. The promise of a high school certificate and better employability outside wasn't enough to lure them away from longer yard periods. Leopold and Loeb found a solution. Both had taken correspondence courses, so now they approached the Bureau of Correspondence Studies at Iowa State University and asked for help. They got it, and Statesville gained an in-house correspondence school for its inmates.

Despite his crimes Loeb's family did not entirely abandon him in prison. Every month he received an allowance of $50 and in the closed small-scale economy of a prison that went a long way. Loeb distributed much of the money among his fellow inmates, buying them tobacco and snacks and Loeb influence. Early in 1936, though, a new warden took over at Stateville and set out to tighten things up. Among the changes he made was to reduce the maximum allowance for convicts to $3 a week, a quarter of what Loeb had been getting. There was nothing he could do about it but violent criminals are not always the most rational of people, and one of them blamed Loeb. James E. Day, Loeb's cellmate, resented the loss of income and lashed out furiously. On January 28, 1936 he ducked out of the lunch line and into the showers, and attacked Loeb with a straight razor.35 Fifty wounds were delivered in a frenzied assault and Loeb was left bleeding copiously on the floor. Prison doctors fought a losing battle against shock and massive blood loss, and within hours of the attack the killer of Bobby Franks was himself dead. Day claimed that Loeb had made an aggressive proposition to him, and despite the fact that Loeb's throat had been cut from behind his version of events was accepted. Day was found not guilty of murder and served out his sentence.

Leopold, not so extrovert as his partner, attracted less attention inside Stateville. He escaped the violence that ended Loeb's life, but afterwards helped wash his body. Then he went on with his sentence. While in prison he took every opportunity to learn, and added another twelve languages to the 15 he already spoke.1 He also studied mathematics and kept on working in the prison school. He raised canaries. In 1944 he volunteered for the Stateville Penitentiary Malaria Study, in which 441 inmate volunteers were deliberately infected with malaria then used to test new antimalarial drugs.36

Leopold was getting by in prison, but he never accepted that he'd spend his whole life

---

[1] There are questions about Leopold's linguistic abilities. Although he did have knowledge of many languages he may only have had reasonable fluency in five of them. Loeb was reported to be irritated by Leopold's constant boasts about speaking 15 languages.

there. The press was still interested in him and carefully he began working to rehabilitate his image. In 1953 he earned a parole hearing. His application had some support, but also plenty of opposition. The State's Attorney, John Gutknecht, was furious and threw his whole weight against Leopold. The application was turned down and the parole board ruled that he couldn't apply again for twelve years.37 They relented in 1958, though, and Leopold was finally released. He had been in prison for 33 years.

[10]
LATER LIFE

When Leopold walked out of Stateville Penitentiary he was 54 years old and had spent nearly two thirds of his life behind bars. Now he just wanted to live out his life quietly. That wouldn't be possible in the center ring of a media circus, so he decided to abandon the USA and move to Puerto Rico. Once there he studied for a sociology degree at the University of Puerto Rico. He worked at various jobs, and also had royalty income; in 1958 he'd published his story, Life Plus Ninety-Nine Years.

Leopold also returned to his old passion, ornithology. Puerto Rico has a rich collection of bird life, with a total of 349 species found there, and he wrote a paper on them. A couple of years after his release Leopold met Trudi Garcia de Quevedo, the widow of a doctor from Baltimore. They married in 1961.

Leopold frequently returned to Chicago to see old friends. When there he would wander the neighborhoods near the university and visit the graves of his parents and two brothers. Most of those connected with the crime had died or left the city, but its notoriety lived on in books and cinema. Perhaps he dreamed of settling back in the old neighborhood, but some wounds healed only slowly. Every visit ended with his return to Puerto Rico.

He never forgot Loeb. In an interview in 1960, a year before his marriage, he told a journalist that he was still deeply in love with him. Several visitors to his home in Puerto Rico commented on the photographs prominently on display. One was Clarence Darrow - "The man who saved my life." The other was Richard Loeb.

On August 20, 1971 Nathan Leopold was hospitalized due to diabetes. Ten days later he died of a heart attack with his wife at his side. After his death his corneas were removed and transplanted into two recipients.38

Conclusion

Even without the confessions the case against Leopold and Loeb was now solid. They'd thought their plan would put them beyond suspicion; instead all it had done was create dozens of chances for the police to confirm pieces of the jigsaw. The list of people who recognized them was growing by the day. The state had no shortage of witnesses to choose from:

Nearly 90 years later Richard Loeb and Nathan Leopold, and the death of Bobby Franks, still exert a strange fascination. They had it all, but wanted more - the thrill of the forbidden.

Their crime has lost its uniqueness and been joined by a depressing list of thrill killings. Jesse McAllister and Bradley Price murdered a couple on a New Jersey beach in 1997 to experience murder. Todd Rizzo, aged 18, killed a 13-year-old with a sledgehammer the same year. 1997 was a bad year, in fact, especially for New Jersey; Thomas Koskovitch and Jayson Vreeland ordered a pizza then ambushed and killed the deliverymen, just to see what killing felt like. There have been crimes when everyone involved was so young it defies belief; in 1993 two English ten-year-olds, Robert Thompson and Jon Venables, abducted toddler James Bulger, molested him then bludgeoned him to death. The catalogue is horrific and grows longer every year. There's something about Leopold and Loeb, though. Maybe it's their high social class, or their intelligence. Their atrocities contrast with the fact that they were also capable of enormous good when they wanted - Loeb once injured a woman in a car accident and persuaded her father to pay all her medical fees, the outstanding loan on her house and a vacation to restore her nerves, and the school system they set up gave hundreds of convicts a chance of turning their lives around. They had every advantage anyone could ask for in life, but faced with a choice opted for nihilistic violence.

Perhaps it's the combination of their personalities that interests us. It's not unusual for nutcases to egg each other on to greater violence, but the Leopold and Loeb case goes beyond that. Both of them were psychologically flawed and disturbingly amoral, but individually it's not likely either of them was capable of murder. Put them together, though, and they exactly cancelled out each other's conscience. They were two halves of a bomb core that, put together, reached a critical mass of psychosis. Bobby Franks wasn't singled out for any reason that would make sense to anyone; he was just standing too close when the bomb went off.

Or maybe we're just drawn to the case by the artists who've shaped our ideas of it. The cell doors had barely slammed on the killers when the first playwright put pen to paper. Patrick Hamilton published Rope in 1929; it was turned into one of the first BBC television plays in 1939 and filmed again by Alfred Hitchcock in 1948. Meyer Levin's Compulsion came out in 1956 and was filmed three years later; the film upset Leopold so much that he tried unsuccessfully to block it, on grounds of invasion of privacy. Never The Sinner hit the theaters in 1988. Other works inspired by it include Swoon, Native Son, Murder By Numbers, Thrill Me: The Leopold and Loeb Story and Funny Games. As long as new adaptations come out the memory of the crime will never fade. Then again, considering the lessons it has for us about what happens when society's rules break down, do we really want it to?

READY FOR MORE?

We hope you enjoyed reading this series. If you are ready to read similar stories, check out other books in the *Stranger Than Fiction* series:

THE TRUE STORY BEHIND ALFRED HITCHCOCK'S PSYCHO

For movie buffs Alfred Hitchcock will always be associated with a long list of Hollywood classics. Between 1921 and 1976 the English director known as the Master of Suspense released 52 feature films, many of which are still thrilling new audiences today. To most people, though, he's best known for a film that was very different – Psycho.

The most fascinating part of movie, however, is actually the real story behind it. This book tells the chilling true story behind of the movie.

THE TRUE STORY BEHIND ALFRED HITCHCOCK'S THE BIRDS

The Birds was different from most of Hitchcock's work. For admirers of Hitchcock The Birds also raises disturbing questions about the director as a person. He was a complex and confusing character in many ways, and perhaps it's not surprising that someone who built a career out of creating suspense and fear on screen might also have had some darker sides to his personal life.

Beyond the details of the story and how it came to be filmed, though, one of the most interesting questions about The Birds is why Hitchcock made it in the first place. It took its title from a short story by English author Daphne du Maurier, but beyond the basic idea of people being attacked by birds it didn't take much else from it. The storyline was pure Hitchcock. So where did it come from?

It turns out that his inspiration was a strange and alarming incident that happened just a few miles from his home in California. This book uncovers the truth behind the plot as well as other factoids that fascinate any fan of the film.

Exposing Jack the Stripper: A Biography of the Worst Serial Killer You've Probably Never Heard Of

Jack the Ripper may get all the fame, but his 1960s counterpart, Jack the Stripper, will really send shivers down your spine. At least six women, all prostitutes, were murdered at his hand--possibly more. Most intriguing of all...he was never caught.

The crimes, though often forgotten today, inspired the crime novel "Goodbye Piccadilly, Farewell Leicester Square," which Alfred Hitchcock turned into the 1972 movie, "Frenzy."

Go inside the hunt for this brutal killer in this gripping short biography.

THE SAPPHIRE AFFAIR: THE TRUE STORY BEHIND ALFRED HITCHCOCK'S TOPAZ

In October 1962 it looked to millions of people like the politicians of the United States and Russia were determined to push the other across the fatal line of launching a nuclear strike. The fate of the world hung on Cuba, a troubled island state in the Caribbean.

Woven through the dramatic events in and around Cuba was a quieter but perhaps equally dangerous scandal – an enormous, deeply embedded network of Soviet spies at the heart of the NATO alliance.

A senior KGB defector had revealed that his agency had penetrated the highest levels of the French government, military and intelligence services – but when a French agent tried to act he found himself blocked at every turn by his own superiors.

Alfred Hitchcock was so impressed by the fictional novel about the events (Topaz by Leon Uris) that he decided to adapt it into a movie. But fiction, as is often the case, only got half of the story. This book tells the remarkable true account of one of the greatest espionage scandals to rock the Cold War.

THE TRUE STORY BEHIND ALFRED HITCHCOCK'S THE WRONG MAN

The Wrong Man tells the incredible tale of an innocent man falsely accused of a crime. That in itself is hardly an unusual story, but in this case a string of unlikely coincidences and sheer bad luck built a seemingly airtight case against him. It seemed that the entire justice system was deaf to his pleas and all too willing to ignore the evidence his defenders had worked so hard to unearth. In the end it was only a slip by the real perpetrator that proved his innocence.

While the movie certainly had it's share of truth, it was still a movie, and parts were fabricated. This book tells the real story behind the movie.

Newsletter Offer

Don't forget to sign up for your newsletter to grab your free book:

http://www.absolutecrime.com/newsletter

Notes

[1] LEOPOLDandLOEB.COM, *Leopold*

[2] LEOPOLDandLOEB.COM, *Leopold*

[3] Hannon, Michael, *The Leopold and Loeb Case*

[4] University of Missouri-Kansas School of Law, *Nathan Leopold and Ornithology*

[5] LEOPOLDandLOEB.COM, *Loeb*

[6] LEOPOLDandLOEB.COM, *Leopold*

[7] Never The Sinner, *The Case and Trial*

[8] Smithsonian Magazine, August 2008, *Leopold and Loeb's Criminal Minds*, Simon Baatz

[9] *Statement of Richard Albert Loeb*, May 31, 1924

[10] Crimerack.com, *Leopold and Loeb Case File*

[11] TruTV.com Crime Library, *Leopold & Loeb*, Marilyn Bardsley, pp. 6

[12] *Statement of Richard Albert Loeb*, May 31, 1924

[13] Hannon, Michael, *The Leopold and Loeb Case*

[14] Journal of the American Institute of Criminal Law and Criminology, 1924, *Loeb-Leopold Case*, pp. 352

[15] *Statement of Richard Albert Loeb*, May 31, 1924

[16] Journal of the American Institute of Criminal Law and Criminology, 1924, *Loeb-Leopold Case*, pp. 353

[17] Journal of the American Institute of Criminal Law and Criminology, 1924, *Loeb-Leopold Case*, pp. 355

[18] LEOPOLDandLOEB.COM, *Apprehension and Interrogation*

[19] *Email from G.M.F to Prof. D. Linder*, July 9, 2011

[20] University of Missouri-Kansas School of Law, *The Glasses: The Key Link to Leopold and Loeb*

[21] Never The Sinner, *The Case and Trial*

[22] Journal of the American Institute of Criminal Law and Criminology, 1924, *Loeb-Leopold Case*, pp. 357

[23] TruTV.com Crime Library, *Leopold & Loeb*, Marilyn Bardsley, pp.8

[24] TruTV.com Crime Library, *Leopold & Loeb*, Marilyn Bardsley, pp.7

[25] The New York Times, Oct 28, 1894, *ASSASSINATED: Carter H. Harrison, Mayor of Chicago, Killed. MURDERER IN CUSTODY*

[26] TruTV.com Crime Library, *Leopold & Loeb*, Marilyn Bardsley, pp. 8

[27] Philly.com, *The defender of the underdog*, John A. Farrell

[28] TruTV.com Crime Library, *Leopold & Loeb*, Marilyn Bardsley, pp. 9

[29] TruTV.com Crime Library, *Leopold & Loeb*, Marilyn Bardsley, pp. 10

[30] TruTV.com Crime Library, *Leopold & Loeb*, Marilyn Bardsley, pp. 8

[31] University of Missouri-Kansas School of Law, *Excerpts from the Psychiatric ("Alienist") Testimony in the Leopold and Loeb Hearing*

[32] Never The Sinner, *The Case and Trial*

[33] University of Missouri-Kansas School of Law, *The Leopold and Loeb Trial: A Brief Account*

[34] Never The Sinner, *The Case and Trial*

[35] MKstage.com, *Loeb*

[36] Time Magazine, Apr 07, 1958, *Books: Condemned to Life*

[37] *Nathan F. Leopold Jr. - Parole Rejection Letter*, May 20, 1953

[38] University of Missouri-Kansas School of Law, *The Leopold and Loeb Trial: A Brief Account*

www.ingramcontent.com/pod-product-compliance
Lightning Source LLC
Chambersburg PA
CBHW020300030426
42336CB00010B/842